CANALETTO: Paintings, Drawings and Etchings

Giovanni Antonio
Canal (Canaletto)
(Engraving by Antonio
Visentini, after
G. B. Piazzetta, 1735)

CANALETTO

Paintings, Drawings and Etchings selected and introduced by

GREGORY MARTIN

THE FOLIO SOCIETY · LONDON · MCMLXVII

List of Plates

Acknowledgements

The publishers wish to thank the following for permission to reproduce their works
and for supplying material from which the reproductions have been made.

By Gracious Permission of Her Majesty Queen Elizabeth II: 3, 8, 9, 35, 37,
38, 42, 43, 44, 45, 46, 48, 49, 50, 51, 62
Alnwick Castle: His Grace The Duke of Northumberland: 21
Arundel Castle: His Grace The Duke of Norfolk: 29
Bowhill: His Grace The Duke of Buccleuch: 24
Cincinnati: Art Museum: 19
Darmstadt: Hessisches Landesmuseum: 34
Goodwood: Trustees of the Goodwood Collection: 4, 5, 23
Hamburg: Hamburger Kunsthalle: 55
Houston, Texas: Museum of Fine Arts, Robert Lee Blaffer Memorial
Collection: 6
London: The Trustees of the British Museum: 33, 47, 53, 54, 56, 57, 58, 59, 60, 61
        Dulwich College Picture Gallery: 26
        The Hallsborough Gallery: 28
        The Trustees of the National Gallery: 7, 16, 17, 18, 25, 27, 30, 31
Lennoxlove: His Grace The Duke of Hamilton and Brandon: 22
Lugano: Baron Thyssen, Schloss Rohoncz Collection: 1
Montreal: Museum of Fine Arts: 32
New York: Pierpont Morgan Library: 52
Oxford: The Ashmolean Museum: 36
Ottawa: National Gallery of Canada: 20
Paris: Louvre: 2
Venice: Gallerie dell'Accademia: 39, 40, 41
Washington, D. C.: National Gallery of Art, gift of Mrs Barbara Hutton: 14, 15
Woburn Abbey: Duke of Bedford: 10, 11, 12, 13
Some of the titles and sizes of the material reproduced and the description of the media
of the drawings are taken from W. G. Constable, *Canaletto*, 2 vols., 1962, to
which the reader is referred for a full discussion of Canaletto's life and art.

Canaletto

Introduction

After a century of obscurity, Venice in the eighteenth century once again became one of the most important artistic centres in Europe. Giovanni Battista Tiepolo is one of the greatest figure painters of all time and he and a host of lesser Venetian artists were in demand as decorators all over Europe. Venice herself was in demand as well, for after Rome, she was the most popular tourist attraction in Italy. In these circumstances a Venetian artist—Canaletto—chose his native city as his main subject-matter and became the greatest view painter in the history of art.

Canaletto's narrow interests naturally set his art apart from the all-embracing scope of the Venetian figure painters. But he shared with them a common basic attitude. For he was an optimist; his vision has a brightness and clarity which bear all the marks of a consciousness that the human condition is tolerable and that the compass of man's soul can be charted. The sun usually shines in his pictures and although he dedicated his life to the accurate depiction of identified views, the result was always an ideal. We can recognize the subject; but we also recognize that it is rendered as art, which makes it better and more perfect than it is.

He was primarily concerned with obtaining visually accurate records of what he saw. At the lowest his skill was a topographer's, at the highest his art was a 'scene maker's'. It is therefore relevant that Giovanni Antonio Canal (called Canaletto) was the son of a theatrical set designer and was trained in his father's profession. Little is known about his father, but the family of da Canal was of noble origin, which, by Canaletto's birth in 1697, was part of a class, close to, but distinct from the Venetian patrician class. The family had property in Venice. Nothing is known of his training; the first that is heard of him, after the record of his birth, is in Rome about 1719–20, preparing the sets with his father for two operas by Scarlatti.

Canaletto was soon to abandon his father's profession. Henceforth his theatre was to be for the most part his native city—Venice—itself a work of art that provides an overwhelming experience for any visitor. Venice gave Canaletto many scenes: squares (campi) and canals lined with Gothic, Renaissance and Baroque churches and palaces. And it is barely a tribute to the freshness of his vision that he found a constant source of inspiration in these surroundings. Such surroundings demanded a recorder; but Canaletto was genius enough not to fill only this requirement. For he had not only a sure sense for architectural detail and perspective, but also (in his youth) a feeling for the atmosphere and life of Venice. Thus his work is as much a record of the scene as the place: he depicted Venice and Venetian life.

Canaletto's training as a set designer would have taught him an important skill: the ranging of buildings in sharp perspective to create an illusion of depth. It would also have given him the kind of vision which sees the person dominated by his surroundings: set designers from Inigo Jones onwards have seen actors dwarfed by their creations. Canaletto had abandoned his craft probably by 1722; certainly by 1725 he had embarked on his career as a view painter by which he was to attain fame and, for some time, prosperity.

View painting, or as often in Canaletto's case, cityscapes, had a relatively short tradition in 1725. For the last hundred years Netherlandish artists had often depicted scenes of city life, but rarely had an artist devoted himself to this genre exclusively. The beauty of Venice had long attracted artists. To a great extent Carpaccio's urban backgrounds are thus inspired and throughout the sixteenth century a view of Venice occasionally makes its appearance in a religious and historical scene. And in the following century, several minor artists painted scenes of Venice's public life, although little is known of their work.

The careers of two artists, however, form the ripple which was to turn into the wave of Canaletto's career.

The eldest was Gaspar van Wittel, a Dutchman, who settled in Italy in 1672 and remained there until his death in 1736. He was active for the most part in Rome, but he executed several views of Venice, two of which, at least, date from the early part of the eighteenth century. The second was an Italian, Luca Carlevaris, to whom Canaletto's art is the most closely related. Carlevaris settled in Venice in 1679 and he died there in 1730. He concentrated on the centre of Venice for his cityscapes and, like his predecessors, painted several episodes in the city's annual cycle of festivities.

It has been suggested that Carlevaris did much to create the taste to which Canaletto so magnificently ministered. In his art, large crowds are massed on the Molo or in the Piazza, and the gorgeous visual drama which Venice could uniquely provide is hinted at. It is not known who were Carlevaris's chief clients; but when he painted, *ca.* 1707/8, two moments in the embassy of the sixth Earl of Manchester he made a link that in the case of Canaletto was to become a chain. The two pictures were probably painted for the Earl himself; and the majority of Canaletto's clients were to be non-Venetians and mostly English. Indeed his most avid admirer was an Englishman, resident in Venice, who became his country's consul there in 1744, Joseph Smith. Smith acted not only as an agent for prospective English patrons of Canaletto, but collected a large group of his works from the late '20s to the early '50s. This collection was sold by him to George III soon after 1760: it contained 54 pictures and 142 drawings by Canaletto.

Canaletto was in great demand in Venice until the early 1740s. Smith's correspondence shows how long some would-be clients had to wait for the master's work. There has been some discussion as to whether Canaletto returned to Rome in the early 1740s, when he produced some Roman views. These are connected with a group of drawings that are thought to have been made by Canaletto when he was in Rome in his youth. The artist's change of subject-matter was symptomatic of a state of affairs, which accounted for his departure from Venice to England in 1746; for the war of the Austrian Succession had cut off the stream of visitors to the city on whom he had relied for commissions.

It was natural that Canaletto should have chosen England to maintain his prosperity. But although he worked for eminent clients, his time spent in England was not without difficulties. He had to contend with rumours that he was not the true Canaletto; such rumours, it has been suggested, were put about by dealers selling imitations of his work, nevertheless they also reflected a falling-off in the artist's powers. For his style was becoming more rigid and stereotyped. The artist twice returned to Venice during his stay in England, and finally returned there soon after 1755.

Canaletto's popularity was now on the decline, although his fame was established. He failed to gain election to the Venetian Academy at his first attempt early in 1763, but succeeded at the next vacancy later in the same year. Also in the same year he was elected Prior of the *Collegio dei Pittori*. He died five years later. Although reputed to have returned from England a rich man, his estate shows the extent of his reduced circumstances at his death.

It is hardly surprising that his powers should have fallen off in his last years. The repetition of similar views, the painful discipline which his art required—with the demands on patience and concentration—would inevitably make any artist not gifted with great genius, and Canaletto was not, mechanical. Occasionally he had broken away from his regular subject-matter and painted other views of other cities; he had also, but more rarely, broken away from reality to create *capricci*—imaginary views. Nevertheless the core of his art was in Venice and to this city he constantly paid homage—the homage, in the last decade or so of his life, of a tired and ageing lover.

The Paintings

Considering the degree to which he was patronized by the English, Canaletto could feel himself hard done by the lack of perceptive comment about his work coming from Englishmen of the time. It was, in fact, a Frenchman and an Italian who best summed up his achievement: the *Président* des Brosses in 1739 wrote that his art was clear, gay, lively and admirable in detail; and Orlandi in 1753 wrote that the eye was deceived [before one of his pictures] into believing that it saw the actual view rather than the picture itself. Liveliness and truth to observable fact are the two chief qualities of Canaletto's art.

Although his patrons may have commissioned Canaletto for the most humdrum of motives—namely to obtain an accurate topographical record—they got much more than this. For he had an amazing, magpie eye for detail of all kinds, whether for the accurate placing of a window or for a figure standing in a gondola. In this sense he was an insatiable visual diarist, who never missed a nuance or inflection. His work is never dull, for it pullulates with fascinating trivia.

The way Canaletto described this trivia also fascinates. His brush was always generously loaded with oil paint and he handled it with a delicious, tricksy facility. Further, his sense of colour was never muddy or ambiguous. As with his fellow-Venetians, his colours are rich and sonorous; and he sought always to give each object its intrinsic colour value. His favourite support was canvas. But he never allowed the weave to obtrude; he always built up his paint to create a thick, succulent surface on which he later came to perform his highly individual visual tricks as the finishing touch.

Canaletto's painted *œuvre* amounts to nearly five hundred works, and a satisfactory explanation of the evolution of his style has only been advanced comparatively recently. He rarely dated a work and historians have had to rely on external evidence such as topographical data, documents and engravings. And although the dating of some important items is still disputed, the disputes only centre round a bracket of a few years—the general line of his development being no longer in doubt.

His earliest views of Venice show him already to have been a master of his skills. There is no hesitation or sense of conflict in the *Piazza San Marco* (no. 1), which must date from before or about 1723 when the paving stones of the Piazza were relaid in their present form. The shadows here are clearly defined to create an almost theatrical effect, and the horses above the entrance to the Basilica stand out against a mysterious and dramatic darkness, while the figures on the Piazza have a certain spidery quality.

In about 1726 his style took on a greater breadth and assurance; perhaps the study of contemporary figure painters gave his own figures a new physical liveliness; at the same time the buildings take on more weight and monumentality. In a group of six large pictures of views near the Piazza, painted for Joseph Smith, he caught, for the only time, the essence of a seaport day: bright and blustery with figures going about their business beneath towering buildings and large skies. In the *Piazzetta towards the Torre dell'Orologio* (no. 3) the paint is laid on with ravishing freedom and ease. The handling is more controlled in his masterpiece of the 'Stonemason's Yard' (no. 7), painted probably a little before 1730. Here Canaletto takes us behind the façade of Venice where there is no parade or display. Washing hangs out beside the Scuola della Carità across the Grand Canal, and in the foreground masons are at work hewing stone that will perhaps embellish a building, thus making it more worthy of holding the stage itself in Canaletto's art. The scene on the left where a mother rushes to gather her fallen child shows Canaletto discarding the mask of the tourist guide and revealing, for one rare moment, a human side.

The mask was reassumed with gusto in a series of views painted for Smith about 1730 and engraved in 1735; twelve were of the Grand Canal, and similar views occur in the series of twenty-four pictures painted for the Duke of Bedford about the same time. This series shows Canaletto at the height of his powers and the effect is one of restrained, yet serene, beauty. Both series included two festival scenes. Smith's were the artist's first renderings of those frequent and lavish displays that commemorated Venice's past glories. The *Regatta on the Grand Canal* (no. 9), where gondolieri race past the carnival platform on the left, catches the glittering splendour of the day and, in the gestures of the onlookers in the foreground, the excitement of the race. More solemn and splendid is the *Bucintoro returning to the Molo* (no. 8). The day is Ascension Day, when the Doge in his magnificent boat, propelled by two hundred oarsmen, set out for the mouth of the Lido where he performed the ceremony of wedding Venice to the sea.

A festival, which Canaletto painted only once, about 1735, was the annual visit of the Doge to the Chiesa di San Rocco to commemorate Venice's deliverance from the plague in 1576. The picture in the National Gallery (no. 16) shows the Doge leaving the church and, accompanied by city officials, processing past the Scuola di San Rocco, on which were displayed, for the occasion, paintings by contemporary masters. Here we are brought closest to participation in the official life of the city; the plague was still a looming presence, and the scene seems to have been composed to emphasize the real significance of the occasion.

The *Basin of San Marco on Ascension Day* (no. 17) was probably painted about 1740 and is far removed from the picture owned by Smith of the same subject. For here beneath a bright sky, Canaletto created a delicious embroidered confectionery where the spectators, massed before the Doge's Palace, are literally like 'hundreds and thousands', and the ripples on the water like thin streaks of icing sugar. Painted a little later and probably shortly before Canaletto's departure for England is *S. Giacomo di Rialto* (no. 20), which already has all the characteristics of the master's final manner. The figures are painted with an easy dexterity, almost by rote; the highlights under the arcade and on the Rialto in the distance are like artificial pearls. These and the visually witty figures give life to the masterly, yet straightforward execution of the buildings.

Many critics see a falling-off in Canaletto's powers from the 1740s; but nevertheless his response at the age of fifty to the challenge that England presented is a tribute to his eye and vision. Certainly his style had become mannered and formalized—even rigid compared with his technique of the 1720s. But his mannerisms have a delightful witticism of their own. His approach to the jagged, overgrown silhouette of *Alnwick Castle* (no. 21) is inevitably tentative: he could hardly have felt at ease in the bleakness of this border country. Nevertheless he found an echo of Venice in the majestic sweep of the *Thames and City of London from Richmond House* (no. 23) where the line of waterside houses and churches carry on into a luminous distance that sparkles with detail. It may be that his figures are no more than symbolic blobs of society, but no one else at the time could render with such fluid ease the raised terrace on the left or pick out with such detail the broad expanse of *Whitehall: Looking to the North, from the vicinity of Montagu House* (no. 24).

Canaletto found release from the severe discipline and dedication to truth which his work required by painting imaginary views often compounded from different architectural features that he knew so well. Such caprice views are rare in his *œuvre*; a few were painted before his departure to England. In 1754 he painted an 'English' caprice view made up out of a building he had already painted—Eton College—and the *Sluice on a River, with a reminiscence of Eton College Chapel* (no. 28) shows the least pretentious side of Canaletto's personality, where he worked as his fancy took him.

Canaletto's production declined after his final return to Venice; now more than ever he saw his subject in terms of a shorthand of blobs and squiggles. But a lively delicacy survived: and a few late works such as the *Piazza San Marco and the Colonnade of the Procuratie Nuove* (no. 31) show that he retained a sure sense of line, a steady, deft hand and a perceptive eye for detail till the end of his career. But they also exemplify what had long been endemic: that his style had become a private language whose often repeated witticisms were bound to grow hollower as he had less and less inclination to find something new to say.

1   Venice: The Piazza San Marco
Oil on canvas, 56 × 80¾ in, Schloss Rohoncz coll., Lugano

2   Venice: The Entrance to the Grand Canal
Oil on canvas, $48\frac{7}{8} \times 83\frac{7}{8}$ in, Musée du Louvre, Paris

3
Venice: The
Piazzetta towards
the Torre
dell'Orologio
Oil on canvas, 67 × 52 in,
H.M. The Queen

4   Venice: The Grand Canal looking North from near the Rialto Bridge
Oil on copper, $18\frac{1}{8} \times 23$ in, The Goodwood Collection

5   Venice: The Grand Canal with the Rialto Bridge from the North
Oil on copper, 18×23 in, The Goodwood Collection

6   Venice: The Entrance to the Grand Canal
Oil on canvas, $19\frac{1}{2} \times 28\frac{1}{2}$ in, Museum of Fine Arts, Houston, Texas

7 Venice: The Campo S. Vidal and Sta. Maria della Carità (The Stonemason's Yard)
Oil on canvas, $48\frac{3}{4} \times 64\frac{1}{8}$ in, The National Gallery, London

8   Venice: The Bucintoro returning to the Molo
Oil on canvas, $30\frac{1}{4} \times 49\frac{1}{2}$ in, H.M. The Queen

9 Venice: Regatta on the Grand Canal
Oil on canvas, $30\frac{1}{4} \times 49\frac{1}{2}$ in, H.M. The Queen

10   Venice: The Grand Canal towards the Palazzo Corner-Spinelli
Oil on canvas, $18\frac{1}{2} \times 31$ in, The Duke of Bedford, Woburn Abbey

11   Venice: The Grand Canal towards the Palazzo Contarini dagli Scrigni
Oil on canvas, $18\frac{1}{2} \times 31\frac{1}{2}$ in, The Duke of Bedford, Woburn Abbey

12 Venice: The Water Entrance of the Arsenal
Oil on canvas, $18\frac{1}{2} \times 31\frac{1}{2}$ in, The Duke of Bedford, Woburn Abbey

13 Venice: The Campo S. Stefano
Oil on canvas, $18\frac{1}{2} \times 31\frac{1}{2}$ in, The Duke of Bedford, Woburn Abbey

14 Venice: The Quay of the Piazzetta
Oil on canvas, signed, 45 × 60¼ in, National Gallery of Art, Washington D.C.

15   Venice: The Piazza San Marco
     Oil on canvas, 45 × 60½ in, National Gallery of Art, Washington D.C.

16   Venice: The Feast Day of S. Roch
      Oil on canvas, $58\frac{1}{8} \times 78\frac{1}{2}$ in, The National Gallery, London

17 Venice: The Basin of San Marco on Ascension Day
Oil on canvas, 48 × 72 in, The National Gallery, London

18 Venice: The upper Reaches of the Grand Canal with S. Simeone Piccolo
Oil on canvas, 49 × 80½ in, The National Gallery, London

19　Rome: The Arch of Septimius Severus with SS. Martina and Luca
Oil on canvas, $20\frac{1}{2} \times 27\frac{1}{2}$ in, Art Museum Cincinnati

20 Venice: S. Giacomo di Rialto
Oil on canvas, 46¾ × 50¾ in, The National Gallery of Canada, Ottawa

21 Alnwick Castle, Northumberland
Oil on canvas, $44\frac{3}{4} \times 55$ in, The Duke of Northumberland, Alnwick Castle

22 London: The Thames from the Terrace of Somerset House, Westminster Bridge in the distance
Oil on canvas, 16 × 27¾ in, The Duke of Hamilton and Brandon, Lennoxlove

23 London: The Thames and City of London from Richmond House
Oil on canvas, 41¾ × 46¼ in, The Goodwood Collection

24   Whitehall: Looking to the North, from the vicinity of Montagu House
Oil on canvas, $46\frac{3}{4} \times 93\frac{1}{2}$ in, The Duke of Buccleuch, Bowhill

25 Eton College
Oil on canvas, $24\frac{1}{4} \times 42\frac{3}{8}$ in, The National Gallery, London

26   Old Walton Bridge
Oil on canvas, recorded as being signed and dated 1754 on reverse, $18\frac{1}{4} \times 29\frac{1}{2}$ in, Dulwich Gallery, London

27   London: Ranelagh, interior of the Rotunda
Oil on canvas, recorded as being signed and dated 1754 on reverse, 18½ × 29¾ in, The National Gallery, London

28   Capriccio: A Sluice on a River, with a reminiscence of Eton College Chapel
Oil on canvas, signed and dated 1754, 32 × 45½ in, The Hallsborough Gallery, London

29 Capriccio: A round Church, with Renaissance and Gothic Buildings
Oil on canvas, $39\frac{1}{2} \times 57\frac{1}{2}$ in, The Duke of Norfolk, Arundel Castle

30
Venice: The Piazza San Marco
Oil on canvas, $18\frac{1}{4} \times 14\frac{7}{8}$ in,
The National Gallery, London

31
Venice: The Piazza
San Marco and the
Colonnade of the
Procuratie Nuove
Oil on canvas, $18\frac{1}{4} \times 15$ in,
The National Gallery, London

32
Venice: The Interior of the
Basilica of San Marco
Oil on canvas, $16\frac{1}{2} \times 11\frac{1}{2}$ in,
The Museum of Fine Arts,
Montreal

The Drawings

Canaletto's drawings present just as wide a view of the artist's scope as do his paintings. Although there are fewer extant drawings than paintings, the relatively large number that exist serve primarily to emphasize the artist's incredible industry and his determination to work from observed evidence. The majority of his drawings represent his artistic capital; for it was from these sometimes rapid, and often very detailed, studies, done on the spot, that he worked up his canvases. Other drawings, however, were made as ends in themselves and some of these reveal an artist far more sensitive to landscape than is apparent in his pictures. It is noteworthy that these were produced probably in the first half of the 1740s, when Canaletto, the painter, was beginning to flag.

The earliest evidence there is of Canaletto discarding his first profession as a set designer is to be found in a group of drawings, the majority of which are in the British Museum. Their authenticity has been disputed, but the least that can be said for them is that they are copies after Canaletto. These drawings were all of Roman views, and they or the last originals from which they derive must have been made during Canaletto's stay in Rome as a young man. The *Arch of Constantine* (no. 33) and the *Cordonata and the Buildings of the Piazza del Campidoglio, with Sta. Maria d'Aracoeli* (no. 34) are two such views which Canaletto kept by him for later reference. Indeed it was not until the 1740s that he made use of them; the *Arch of Constantine* served as the basis for a painting for Smith which is dated 1742.

The style of these later drawings bears little relation to the fresh and breezy sketches Canaletto made of Venice in the 1720s. In the *Piazza San Marco* (no. 35), executed probably early in the second half of the 1720s, Canaletto after ruling in the main lines of the buildings let his pen nimbly race across the sheet noting the architectural detail and emphasizing the shadow cast by the Procuratie Nuove. The same sense of hurried but clear note-taking is apparent in the *South-west Angle of the Doge's Palace* (no. 36). It was from such drawings as these that the long process of picture making was begun: in them the artist established his main terms of reference and set out his general idea. He was to continue to make such sketches for the rest of his career, but with growing experience they take on a more calm and workmanlike approach. Thus the *Campo S. Stefano* (no. 42) and the *Molo* (no. 43), probably both sketched on the spot, represent a step much closer to the actual process of setting paint to canvas.

With the increase in demand for his work, it must have become obvious to Canaletto that haphazard forays from the studio to take notes were unsatisfactory. In the Gallerie dell'Accademia at Venice there is preserved a complete sketchbook, which is evidence of the artist's determination to have readily available complete records of the architecture of the city. Not all the sketches are in the same medium, but the majority suggest that at one time the artist worked along the Grand Canal, and took in other major buildings, systematically taking detailed notes of what he saw. Thus the two sheets devoted to the *Palazzi Giovanelli and Bembo; Palazzo Bembo* (no. 39) contain colour notes and notes concerning ownership. By turning over the sheets of the sketchbook, Canaletto would have obtained a complete view of the line of the *palazzi* along the Grand Canal. The sketchbook also contains two sheets of rare studies of figures and shipping. It has been suggested that Canaletto must have completed other sketchbooks, now lost, in the same manner; he probably completed this one by about 1730 and had it at hand when he embarked on the series of twenty-two views of Venice commissioned by the Duke of Bedford.

To a much greater extent than the paintings, Canaletto's drawings show how he broadened his scope in the 1740s. In the years immediately before his departure for England, when the demand for views of Venice may well have fallen off, he looked about for other subjects and the stimulus he gained from this change of scene is brilliantly shown in his graphic work. There are in fact more drawings than paintings that show the fruits of his restlessness. As well as views of Rome, perhaps reminiscences, he produced some marvellously worked up views of Padua and some imaginary caprice views. But the highlight of his art at this time are two drawings of the Venetian Lagoon. The *Island of S. Elena, the Lido in the distance* (no. 48) and the *Islands of S. Elena and S. Pietro* (no. 49) have an almost Chinese quality in the hazy, calm stillness achieved with a minimum of fuss. They are utterly personal and timeless statements, far removed in spirit from the type of expression Canaletto was making in paint at the time.

Inevitably these two drawings set a standard by which what preceded and succeeded them appears dull. His drawn views of England are as precise and amusing as his paintings would lead one to expect. But it was on a drawing that the artist set down a unique and moving personal statement concerning his predicament as an old man in his last years. In 1766 he inscribed a drawing he had made of the *Interior of the Basilica of San Marco* (no. 55); it had been drawn 'without spectacles' and the artist noted that fact with pride.

The Etchings

The least known aspect of Canaletto's art is his etchings. He produced thirty of these and dedicated the set to the most devoted of his patrons—Joseph Smith. Exactly when he made them is not certain, nor is it known who taught Canaletto this most delicate and taxing of skills. It is likely that he produced them in the first half of the 1740s, when, as we have seen, he was casting about to enlarge his scope to make good the probable decline in demand for pictures of Venetian views. The set of thirty prints is a remarkable tribute to the success of this endeavour and reveals a delightful aspect of his limited genius.

The set includes identified views (of Padua, Mestre, Dolo, the Venetian Lagoon and Venice itself), unidentified views, and imaginary landscapes. These are either capricci with an identifiable monument or purely imaginary—perhaps inspired by the Dolomites. The series show Canaletto to have been a master etcher whether undertaking panoramic views such as '*Pra della Valle*' (no. 58) or '*Ale Porte del Dolo*' (no. 56). But on a higher level *La Torre di Malghera* (no. 59) approaches the achievement of Canaletto's drawings of the Lagoon, while the imaginary landscapes such as the *Mountain Landscape with three Bridges* (no. 60) and the *Landscape with a Church, Mills and a Bridge* (no. 62), of which only two examples are known, have a breathtaking sense of fantasy that owes something to the taste for *chinoiserie*.

33   Rome: The Arch of Constantine
Pen and brown ink with grey wash over pencil, 6 × 8¾ in, British Museum (ascribed to Canaletto)

34　Rome: The Cordonata and the Buildings of the Piazza del Campidoglio, with Sta. Maria d'Aracoeli
Pen and brown ink with grey wash over pencil, 6 × 8¾ in, Darmstadt, Kupferstichkabinett (ascribed to Canaletto)

35 Venice: The Piazza San Marco
Pen and blackish ink, $7 \times 9\frac{1}{4}$ in, H.M. The Queen

36

Venice: South-west
Angle of the Doge's
Palace
Pen and brown ink, $8\frac{7}{8} \times 6\frac{7}{8}$ in,
The Ashmolean Museum,
Oxford

37 Venice: The Riva degli Schiavoni with the Doge's Palace
Pen and bistre over pencil, $7\frac{5}{8} \times 12\frac{1}{8}$ in, H.M. The Queen, Windsor

38   Venice: The Riva degli Schiavoni towards Sta. Maria della Salute in the distance
Pen and brown ink over pencil, 8½ × 12½ in, H.M. The Queen, Windsor

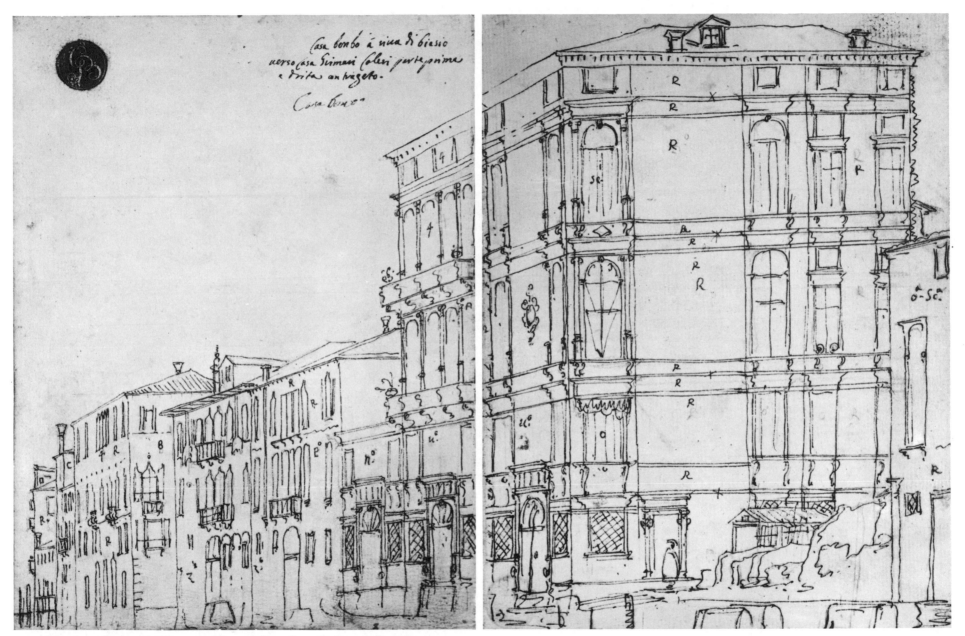

39   Venice: Palazzi Giovanelli and Bembo; Palazzo Bembo
Pen and brown-black ink over black chalk, 9 × 6⅝ in (sheets 47r and 46v of the Canaletto sketchbook in the Gallerie dell'Accademia, Venice)

vista del campo di S. Gio. e Paol. da ca Dandolo
Vesso barbaria dale tole parte prima e drita.

40   Venice: SS. Giovanni e Paolo and Campo SS. Giovanni e Paolo
Pen and brown-black ink over black chalk, $9 \times 6\frac{5}{8}$ in (sheets 51r and 50v of the Canaletto sketchbook in the Gallerie dell'Accademia, Venice)

41   Boats and Barges; Barges and Figure Studies
Pen and brown-black ink over black chalk, 9×6⅝ in (sheets 57v and 58r of the Canaletto sketchbook in the Gallerie dell'Accademia, Venice)

42   Venice: The Campo S. Stefano
Pen and brown-black ink over pencil, $10\frac{5}{8} \times 14\frac{3}{4}$ in, H.M. The Queen, Windsor

43   Venice: The Molo
Pen and brownish-black ink over pencil, $8\frac{7}{16} \times 12\frac{3}{4}$ in, H.M. The Queen, Windsor

44   Rome: The Tiber with the Ponte Rotto and Sta. Maria in Cosmedin
Pen and dark brown ink over pencil, $10\frac{5}{8} \times 14\frac{3}{4}$ in, H.M. The Queen, Windsor

45   Rome: SS. Domenico and Sisto
Pen and black ink over pencil, $7\frac{5}{8} \times 11\frac{1}{8}$ in, H.M. The Queen, Windsor

46 Capriccio: Ruins of a domed Building and a triumphal Arch
Pen and black ink over pencil, $7\frac{13}{16} \times 11$ in, H.M. The Queen, Windsor

47   Imaginary Composition: Ruins and a Bridge by the Lagoon
Pen and brown ink with grey wash over pencil, $9\frac{3}{8} \times 15\frac{1}{8}$ in, British Museum

48 Island of S. Elena, the Lido in the distance
Pen and brown ink with grey wash, $6\frac{1}{8} \times 13\frac{3}{4}$ in, H.M. The Queen, Windsor

49   Islands of S. Elena and S. Pietro
Pen and brown ink with grey wash over pencil, $6\frac{1}{8} \times 13\frac{3}{4}$ in, H.M. The Queen, Windsor

50 Padua: View from the Ramparts with Sta. Giustina
Pen and black ink over pencil, $7\frac{3}{8} \times 10\frac{3}{4}$ in, H.M. The Queen, Windsor

51 Padua: The Ramparts and a City Gate
Pen and brown-black ink over pencil, $7\frac{3}{8} \times 10\frac{5}{8}$ in, H.M. The Queen, Windsor

52   Panoramic View of Houses and Gardens by a River at Padua (?)
Pen and brown-black ink over red chalk, $5\frac{3}{4} \times 15\frac{1}{2}$ in, Pierpont Morgan Library, New York

53 Hampton Court Bridge, Middlesex
Pen and brown ink with grey wash, $9\frac{1}{8} \times 15\frac{5}{16}$ in, British Museum

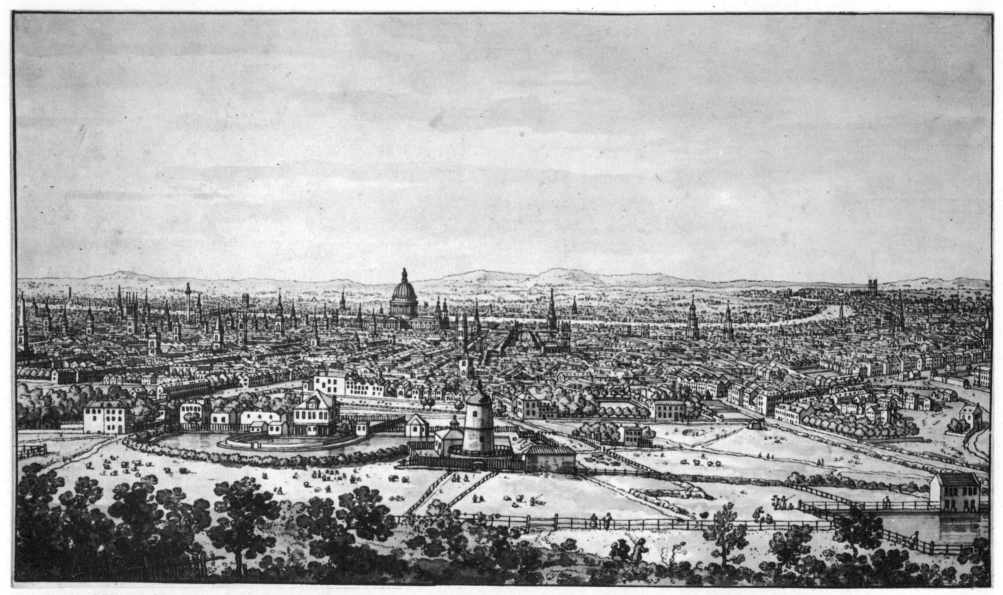

54   General View of London, from Pentonville
Pen and brown ink with grey wash, $9\frac{1}{16} \times 15\frac{5}{8}$ in, British Museum

Io Zuane Antonio da Canal, Hò fatto il presente diseqnio delli Musici che Canta nella Chiesa Ducal di S. Marco in Venezia in età de
Anni 68 Cenzza Ochiali, Lanno 1766.

55
Venice: The Interior of the
Basilica of San Marco
Pen and brown ink and
indian ink wash over
pencil, signed and dated
1766, $18\frac{1}{2} \times 14\frac{1}{8}$ in,
Kunsthalle, Hamburg

A. Canal F.   Ale Porte del Dolo.

56   'Ale Porte del Dolo' (Dolo on the River Brenta)
$11\frac{9}{16} \times 16\frac{11}{16}$ in

57   'Mestre' (Mestre: The Canale delle Barche)
$11\frac{5}{8} \times 16\frac{5}{8}$ in

58   'Pra della Valle' (Padua: The Prato della Valle towards the Chiesa della Misericordia)
11 11/16 × 16 3/4 in

59 'La Torre di Malghera' (The Venetian Lagoon with a view of the Tower of Malghera)
$11\frac{2}{5} \times 16\frac{5}{8}$ in

60 Mountain Landscape with three Bridges
$5\frac{9}{16} \times 8\frac{1}{8}$ in

61 · 'Le Procuratie Niove e S. Ziminian V' (Venice: The Piazza San Marco towards the Procuratie Nuove)
$5\frac{9}{16} \times 8\frac{3}{16}$ in

62   Landscape with a Church, Mills and a Bridge
$5\frac{7}{16} \times 8\frac{1}{4}$ in